Burn it All

An Ekphrastic Novella-in-Flash

Karen Jones

ARROYO SECO PRESS

Editor: LeAnne Hunt

Logo by Morgan G Robles

Arroyo Seco Press

www.arroyosecopress.org

Cover art: cover image by Assad Ali Pixabay

ISBN: 979-8-9895659-3-1

For Alfie, Ross and Aidan, with love.

Contents

Sisters

My sisters have placed the table too close to the sea, the waves rising behind it, like petticoats thrown up in a whirl of dancing. I'm sure they set it there to panic me. A candelabra teeters on the edge of the table, its candles' flames snuffed out by the wind and salty spray, trailing smoke towards the sky, looking like the funnels on the ship that was due to arrive home six days ago—a ship they hope we will never see again, that the storms have taken it and him to the depths. In my depths, even though I don't love him, I still hope for my husband's return, for stability. They say this is my taunt, this fact of my marriage, albeit to a man like him, while they are spinsters. But look at them. Look at my sisters, Esther playing the fiddle, her head at such an awkward angle it seems partially severed, her fingertips hardened by plucking strings instead of chickens, and Olivia dancing, bare-legged, red hair flying with the wind, with wildness, with her joy at the thought of my widowhood. Who would have them? The dogs and gulls fight over the feast on the table, and they are the only ones who eat. I have been given a slice of cake, as though this is a happy day, as though the storm is not rising, as though the darkness is not coming, as though it won't take us all when there is no one to provide. Behind us, our house—his house—is open to the elements, windows thrown wide, curtains dancing to my sister's tune, but it, too, is too close to the sea, tilting on its foundations, tempted to slip away and leave us with nothing. I pull my cape tight around my shoulders to fend off the cold my sisters, the gulls and dogs don't feel, and look away from the sea. If I don't look, it cannot touch us. I wish I could shake the feeling that no one will ever touch me again.

1

Drifting

I imagine myself at sea instead of my husband. He stays here, in this broken-down house, surrounded by the burning fields and my sisters, while I sail to places I have never even heard of. I set my body to sway from side to side as I collect eggs, bake bread, make pies, as though I am on a ship, far from here, struggling to keep my balance. I spin the globe our mother bought, let my fingers settle on countries and cities where I could land and explore and be another me—a me I know exists under aprons and hair clips and flour-covered fingers. I could drink wines and ales, eat strange fruits, hear foreign voices and rejoice in not understanding words, but communicate in only glances, gestures, raised eyebrows. I'm sure I could learn to use that language. I'd have a uniform, lots of buttons and epaulets, though no medals—I do not seek celebration. I only want to exist as another thing—a more useful thing.

My sisters laugh at my fantasies. They know my thoughts and dreams, even though I have never told them of these fancies. They know my mind as if it were theirs. Sometimes I think it is theirs, that they control it, control me, confine me. But I know that is madness. Loneliness has a way of inviting insanity to squat in otherwise sane minds.

I know what I must do to rid myself of these thoughts. I must go out more with my sisters rather than observe their expeditions. They come to the door where I am baking bread and wave their butterfly nets. An invitation they have made before. Next time, maybe.

The Visit

My mother-in-law sends notes, asking to visit. I do not want her here. I have met her only once, the day the marriage was agreed and the papers were signed. She did not attend the wedding — none of his family did. I have never met his father, nor do I wish to. If we are our mother's daughters, then, from what I have heard, he is his father's son.

I send notes back, talking of inconveniences, illnesses, away days, promise I will be in touch about a suitable time. And would it not be better if I came to her? Her house so much nicer. Her servants there to cater for us. But no, she wishes to see me in my marital home.

My sisters laugh when they read that word. 'This is no such thing, Beth. That brute has never been here as a husband.'

This is true. But it is also true that it is now his name — his family name — on the deeds, so I cannot refuse indefinitely.

When she finally comes to tea, to check up on me, my sisters prepare one of their feasts. Some things cooked, some raw, some so raw they still walk around the kitchen, scratching at the dust on the floor. I was sure I had swept, cleaned, dusted, but our open windows and doors mean everything is no sooner clean than it is dirty again. My sisters have made elaborate hair choices — swept up with bows and ribbons and scarves, but still sprouting free at random places. They hold their cups with pinkies arched so far, their tea dribbles onto their skirts or drips to the floor where the dogs slurp it up amidst their scowling jowls.

My mother-in-law doesn't know where to look. When she takes the milk to pour into her tea, a squirrel escapes my sister

Livvie's hold and skitters across the table towards her. She panics, pours the milk onto a guinea pig that has taken up residence in the breadbasket. I smile, smile as though none of this is happening, smile as though she is the strange one. She doesn't stay long — just long enough to ask if there is anything I need until my husband returns, which is kind of her. I tell her everything is fine and that she should call again on a day when I am alone and less distracted. She looks around the room, pats my arm and agrees. When she leaves, my sisters let down their hair and laugh as they gather up the animals. For once, I join in their fun.

There Goes the Bride

Until our wedding day, I had never really looked into his eyes. I saw nothing there—I did not expect to see love, we did not know each other well, but I looked for some speck of kindness, of regret for previous actions, and found none. He barely looked at me at all. This was a transaction rather than a love match. My family's house and fields would become part of his family's land. He had no interest in those things either. He is not a farmer, he is a sailor, and all he wanted was to get back to his true love. My sisters said I should be grateful for this—at least he would not be there on my wedding night to paw at me, to bother me, to hurt me again. But there are different kinds of pain.

My sisters did not attend the wedding, said it was not a real wedding, that they would never take him as a brother. 'We do not need a brother, Beth. We do not need a man to rule over us. We have each other. We have the dogs and the crows to guard us. We have our songs. We have our workers in the fields. We are all we need.'

They are naïve. No one would trade with us. No one trades with women, except to take advantage. And though he will not be here, though he will not be the one at the markets, the crops will bear his name. We need his name.

I looked at him as we finished the vows, his eyes already searching through the window for the sea. He did not offer me his arm, simply turned on his heels, and I followed, scurrying behind him.

No swell of wedding march for me as we left the empty church. We stepped outside, and he was gone, without a word, to his ship. A cloud of crows surrounded me like dark confetti, scattered by the boom of a bird cannon. I let my flowers drop to the ground and trudged across the fields, where my dress, once my mother's, now mended with patches from her lace tablecloths, gathered burrs, tore on barbs. I reached my family's house. Was it still a home now that he had taken it as he had taken me? Alone in my marital bed, I counted my blessings; it did not take long.

Prior Arrangements

Our mother told us of her first visit to this place, already betrothed to our father, although they had never met. She came by train, accompanied only by her dog. As well as her luggage, she carried a small box — a gift for our father. Not part of a dowry, but an expensive watch, our maternal grandfather's way of saying our mother came from something and was not nothing. The journey was long, and she arrived tired. Our father and his parents met her at the station, looked at the dog with suspicion — it was not a working dog, so what use could it be — helped her up onto the cart and took her to the house.

'I fell in love with this place the moment I saw it,' she told us. 'So close to the sea, yet dry and hard and full of russets and greens. It suited me — I felt I could wear it like a fine dress.'

We looked around, thinking her mad. There was nothing fine here — everything was falling apart.

She followed our gaze. 'But that was then. That was when people had money, when we could sell crops at top rates, when our cattle was prized. It was different, before wars. Before everything...'

Everything. Everything being our father's family losing so much of the lands they had owned, of her own father's business crumbling in the recession.

And our father? Did she fall in love with our father? Was that also love at first sight?

'Later,' she said. 'That happened later.'

Father peered over the top of his newspaper when she said that, looked at his watch and smiled.

Strange Creatures

Our mother kept a pheasant as a pet. There is a photograph of her sitting in a chair, the pheasant on a leash. Mother wears a black feather boa, looking like an exotic bird companion for her plainer pet. The pheasant gazes out of the open window, and we are sure it feels confined and wishes to escape, but mother assures us that was never the case. They were devoted to each other, and even when those windows were open and the leash not used, the pheasant never tried to leave. We asked her what she called the pheasant, and she looked confused.

'What name did you give it?' we asked again.

She looked at us as though we had lost our minds. 'It was a pheasant—why would it need any other name?'

When I look at the picture now, all I see are two trapped creatures, feathers fluffed, sitting by an open window, but neither daring to escape. I see myself in my mother and my mother in me, and now I am all that is left.

Preservation

I press flowers. I do not enjoy this hobby, but my sisters like to preserve things, so I do it to indulge them. My friends the bees buzz me while I work. They tell me what I am doing is wrong, that I am killing their food and storing it in a way that benefits no one. But there is plenty of food, I tell them—they should not begrudge me a little piece for nothing more than beauty. But it is not beauty—it is decay, they say. I keep dead things around me and that is not healthy, they say. One of them fake-dies, a little too dramatically, and his brothers ask if I would keep him this way too—press him between the pages of a book, his body flattened, his lifeblood cleaned away for the sake of aesthetics. I would like to say no, but they have seen me join my sisters in butterfly hunts and collecting fireflies in jars, so my protests would not be believed. The hive I have allowed them to make in my bedroom is alive with indignation. I sigh, tell them they are right, promise to stop, but my sisters whisper their encouragement to do as I please.

My dog is quiet today, not snarling or biting. I think he is afraid of the bees, so stays still, hoping they will not notice him. Three bees teeter on the edge of a vase and fall into the water. I could save them. I choose not to.

My sisters say I should not have allowed the hive inside the house, and especially not in my bedroom. But who else is there to sleep with me? Who else is there to care for me? I keep them here and pretend I am their queen, though really I am nothing more than their landlady, requiring only a little honey as payment for their lodgings.

9

The hive reminds me of our mother's hair on the days she would sweep it up and up and up to make us laugh. We never knew we would have that same hair one day. And that same laugh. We are our mother, all three of us, in different ways.

Nothing Like Love

That one night he took me, before we married, still confuses me. I don't know why he did it. He turned up at the house, pushed his way in, cleared the dishes from the floured table and threw me down, pulling at my clothes and his, shoving his way into me, all the while looking out of the window towards the sea. My sisters, who are always under my feet, were nowhere to be seen. If they had been there, they would have stopped him, I'm sure. I prayed for them to arrive. Except I did not need them because he suddenly grew small, stopped, slithered out and away, shaking his head. He turned and left the house and me in disarray. I collapsed to the floor. Livvie and Esther appeared, already knowing what had happened, as somehow they always do. They sat, stroking my hair and raining down curses on his head. All else was silent. The dogs, the chickens, the crows, the insects had all hushed. I stood up, brushed the flour from my skirt, felt the trickle of blood run down my leg.

Was that it? Was that love, or his idea of it? I cleaned myself, my sisters fussing around me, wailing now. I gathered them to me and held them, promised this would never happen to them. I would bear this for all of us. After the wedding he would be gone for most of the time, and given what had occurred and how little pleasure he had taken in it, I doubted there would be many repeat performances.

My sisters dried their tears, said we should go for a walk, get out into the air, blow away his evil. I nodded, but what I really wanted was to curl up in the corner with the dogs and let them heal me, as they always do. Sometimes I wish I could be truly alone.

Day Out to Nowhere-Land

Sometimes I pretend I am leaving this place, mount the cart, sit there with one of my dogs in my lap. Chickens join my daring escape, ride alongside on cartwheels. One has taken to roosting in the hatbox on the seat behind me, safe in the knowledge that we won't be going anywhere, that her eggs will not be shaken over stony roads, will not scramble to their death as we pick up speed, will not be broken by leaving this place. The hatbox and small suitcase are always there on the seat, always packed with inessentials, things I think I would like in another life. In this life, I need sturdy boots, aprons, hair clips, woollen tights and fortitude. In the life away from here I'd have dainty shoes, fancy petticoats, ribbons, silk stockings and peace. The chickens scratch at my knees and feet, feet that twitch to dance with someone other than my sisters. My husband did not dance—did not dance with me, at least. Perhaps he dances in the ports he visits, or with other men on the ship, or on his own, drunk, free and happy in his cabin. Or perhaps his ghost dances at the bottom of the sea with crabs and creatures I cannot even contemplate. Perhaps, if he ever returns, he will dance with me. My sisters say he will not return. They say they know. They say this with smiles and giggles. Their certainty chills me. I pull my cardigan tight around my shoulders; the chickens flutter their clipped wings. I look down the road, know the gate is there, waiting to be opened. I climb down from the cart, shoo the chickens and dreams away and return to the kitchen, to the endless baking, to my sisters.

Knowing and Waiting

In the warm evening air, my sisters dare to remove their aprons and blouses, their shoulders bared, sitting in the field, leaning back, mayflies hovering around their heads, bullfrogs hopping by their hands, the wheat in the field embracing them. I could never be so free as to wear so little outdoors. Not that there is anyone here to see. The men who work in the fields have gone home for the day, so it is just me, my sisters, the dogs, the birds, the insects, our thoughts and fears. My sisters have only one fear, but we do not speak of it. I have a hundred fears, but they have no interest in them. They think me lucky, and I suppose I am, in some ways. Missed chances are my curse, and the fear of no more chances haunts me more than anything else.

On the days when I am convinced my husband is not coming back, that he has drowned, either at sea or in another's arms, I wear black. The crows approve and surround me like both hat and shawl. My sisters smile when they see me this way, liking that I have come round to their way of thinking—to what they say is their absolute knowledge that he is dead. I know how they know. I do. I pretend otherwise. My first thought, if it is true, is to burn it all down—everything here, even the fields. But I cannot do that to my sisters. And what then? Leave, let it all go to ruin? Would my sisters be able to follow me to my next home? And where could that be, with no money, no husband?

My sisters wear lace, play sad songs on their fiddles, but their toes twitch to dance. I tell them to go ahead.

We Used to Have Cows

Just before the barn burned down, I decided to run away. Not properly, not forever—only for that day. That was as much as I had planned. My mother and sisters were in the barn, milking the cows. I was supposed to be in the kitchen, preparing breakfast for the men. I went to the barn, tripped over the stone that held the broken door open, which made my sisters laugh, which made me embarrassed and angry. I don't know why—usually I laugh with my sisters, even if it is at my own expense. I was in an odd mood that day. I collected a pail of fresh milk, kicked away the stone that had contrived to hurt me, took the milk to the kitchen, set it down on the floor, then ran.

I've never known why I chose that day to escape for a while. I left no note, told no one—not even the bees—took no money or food or a warm coat for the evening. I simply ran. I ran through the fields, my chest heaving but expanding more than it had ever done, my lungs soon capable of taking in more and more air. I unclipped my hair, let it fly behind me. My boots felt lighter, like slippers, my cardigan billowed like wings, my smile so wide the wind dried my teeth and my lips stuck to my gums. When I reached the gate, I stopped to take one last look back. That was when I saw the smoke coming from the barn, imagined I could hear the screams, could smell the burning flesh.

I rushed back, helped my father and the men with buckets of water, but it was too late. The screams had stopped. Too late. We never kept cows after that.

Possibilities

Since my husband left for the sea, the men we hired to tend the fields look at me differently. Something like pity, and I am so sick of pity. My sisters pity me when they are not making fun of me. I never know which is worse. The dogs and birds try to take over the house. At first I closed all the windows and doors, but my sisters need the windows and doors open all day and night, curtains flying out into the wind, no matter the weather. We have yet to reach a compromise, our lives an endless round of opening and closing and never quite getting it right.

I used to pity the men, their painful toil for so little return, but now I envy them, envy the burn in their muscles, the sweat on their brows, the dirt that seeps so far into their skin, I imagine them scrubbing in vain to remove it. I stand at the window and watch them work—they never seem to notice—and picture them washing themselves clean. My face burns so much I fear my thoughts have conjured a fire around them, surrounding this house, everything consumed by flames.

One day, one of the men looks up, tilts his hat in my direction, a half-smile on his lips. My sisters, gathering flowers and singing our songs just beneath the window, giggle. Were they watching? Do they know these thoughts? Of course they do. They know all of my thoughts. But they do not have them. They have never felt this way, not having been married. I only had that one, terrible night with him before he left for the sea, and it was rough and painful and never raised a sweat or a love to be washed away. But it made me curious. I long to know real love. I smile back at the worker in the field, though his head is bowed again and he does not see. My sisters fake gasp before dissolving into laughter again. I go back to kneading dough on the table.

Impossibilities

My sisters are not there, are not here. Were they ever real? I think they were, before the fire. I see my mother with them, baking, sewing, tending to the chickens, feeding the dogs. What would they have become? What would I have become had my father not married me off to save the house and the land that was left? What if he had not gone to be with my mother and sisters before the wedding day? What if my husband had married me because he loved me, not this land for his family? What if, what if, what if... What if I call to the man in the field, the one who smiles at me? What if I take him to my bed—the marital bed—what if, by the time my husband comes home, if he ever comes home, I am surrounded by the man's children, red-headed daughters, their hair wild and free, who dance in the fields, but close the windows and doors as they have no fear of being trapped by fire or duty? What if, using the language I would have learned had I been the one to go to sea, with just a glance I bring him in here? What if I offer him fresh bread, water and me? What do I have to lose? If I look out to the man, hold up the loaf, tilt my head to one side, raise one eyebrow, allow my lips to tease a smile, would he lay down his scythe, wipe his brow and walk towards me? If I did these things, if I then became truly happy, would I ever see my sisters again?

A Kinder Light

My sisters still catch fireflies in jars, just as we did when we were children. Back then, our mother placed a piece of damp paper in the bottom of the jars, telling us fireflies like moist air, and only to puncture a couple of holes in the lids so the paper wouldn't dry out too quickly. But we worried about the fireflies, about how they would breathe, how they could live in jars with so little air. Our mother would pat our heads and say, 'It's amazing how some things can exist in captivity—but only for a little while, then you must set them free.'

Dressed in our night clothes, we would run into the fields, with small nets and jars, barefooted, wild children that we were, and capture the tiny creatures. We had competitions to see who had the most, who had the brightest, who could keep them alive longest before they were set free. Back in the kitchen, we'd dim the lights and eat supper at the table, lit only by the fireflies. They'd light our way to bed, and we'd fall asleep watching their beauty, knowing our mother would set them free while we slept.

It's all so long ago, the memory is beginning to fade, like fireflies held too long. But my sisters will always remember. They are the keepers of all our memories.

My sisters still insist on wearing only nightclothes when they go on their hunts. I could never be so daring, even if I weren't a married woman. They have kept their wildness, but mine has been stifled. There is no one now to tell them they have a bedtime, no one to put damp paper in the jars, no one to promise them that the insects don't need a lot of air. I have not, could not, replace our mother. Even if I tried, they would never listen to me. They run from our kitchen, nets held high, hair flying behind them, jars ready to capture all the light that is missing from this house. There are not enough fireflies in the world for that.

Ordinary Families

The men who work in the fields answer only to me. My sisters have no time for such dreariness. They have pies to bake and bread to eat and bugs to catch and reels to dance and dogs to play with and herbs to gather and me to make fun of. It's a full day for them, every day.

Locals used to call our mother a witch. Never to her face, of course. She gathered herbs, knew how to use them for medicine as well as cooking. But that wasn't what marked her out as something to be wary of; it was that wild hair we have inherited. No other women around here have hair like ours, and that is enough to have us deemed odd. We are odd, but it has nothing to do with our hair.

We are odd because we prefer our own family's company. We are odd because, since our parents died, only one of us has married. We are odd because we seem to have no interest in men. We are odd because of the way we dress, the way we speak, the way we dance in storms and play fiddles at fires and allow animals to live in our house. We are odd because we wish to be feral, just like our animals. We are odd because our mother kept a pheasant on a leash and our father never questioned her behaviour.

But we are not odd at all. Not to each other.

Lost at Sea

Last night I slept alone in the field. No covers under or over—just me and the wheat. The dogs did not come to me, no insects bothered me, only me and the night. I dreamt I walked through a field of marigolds to a castle. The castle stood where our house should be. The sea had disappeared, and we were inland. In the castle shone five lights at windows. I knew I had to choose which one to walk towards, knew that in each one of four I would find a sister I loved or my mother or father. But what of the fifth window? I walked on, still unsure of my choice, but the closer I got to the castle, the lights went out, one by one, until a single option remained.

When I reached the castle's walls, the lit window opened, and my husband leant out to look at me. His skin was blue, and seaweed and shells hung from his hair and beard. He grinned, his teeth broken and brown. He laughed as he threw coins down that hit and hurt me, and no matter how much I begged him to stop, still the coins rained down, leaving cuts and bruises on my arms and face.

When I woke, my face covered in marigold petals, I heard a ship's horn, close to the shore. I jumped up and ran to find my sisters, but they were already there, at the cliff's edge, shawls pulled tight around their shoulders, pointing to the boat that had been lowered. Three men rowed towards us, but too far away to make out their faces. We scurried to the kitchen, to tidy, to make ourselves and this place presentable, to make his house look like the home it had never yet been for him. Not that he would care.

When the men left, when we knew for sure that my husband would never return, my sisters danced with joy, but at first, I could take no pleasure in his death. He had hurt me, physically as well as mentally, but I had wondered, once he came home, once we spent time together, could we have found common interests? Could we have liked each other, created a life here?

Livvie took both my hands in hers. 'He was a bad man. An evil man. He hurt you for fun, but even that bored him.'

Esther shook her head. 'You would never have interested him. Women were not to his liking.'

And of course, they were right. I saw it clearly then.

'Set the table again, Livvie,' I said.

She looked confused. 'The way you did that day when you knew he was lost. When you two wanted to celebrate. Now we know he is gone, set the table again, too close to the edge, light the candles, bring the cake. This time, let's do it properly.'

My sisters twirled and birled with glee. A private party. A farewell. A good riddance, for sure. But what then? Would we be allowed to stay on this land? We could worry about that later.

Stranger Creatures

My sisters have brought me a hedgehog. They say it is the perfect pet for me. They say this with laughter, of course. But perhaps they are right—perhaps I have become prickly, nocturnal and unapproachable. Perhaps I always was.

Every day, I place fish on the windowsill for the seagulls. I know I don't have to do this—they are perfectly capable of catching their own fish. And the ones they catch are alive and still flopping, rather than sitting rotting on the windowsill. But I like to watch them attack their food. They used to grab the fish and fly away, but now, used to me and our ritual, they stay and eat by my side. It makes me feel needed. I like that feeling. I thought I hated it. Thought that was what I wanted to escape—this endless drudgery and domesticity, such as it is. My sisters have made it fun and chaotic, but it is still tiresome. Yet I know now that is not the freedom I seek.

The hedgehog sits on my lap, and I am afraid to move in case I disturb it. I read somewhere that you should never touch a hedgehog—that once it has a human's scent on it, its family will abandon it. What does human scent smell like to a hedgehog? Captivity? Death? Or simply failure. It does not matter; it is part of our family now, and I will keep it safe. But my mother was right about such pets—they need no other name. And this one will never be leashed.

The Family Menagerie

Most of the animals have moved into the house now—my sisters like it that way, and I no longer have the energy or desire to fight them. The kitchen is full of chickens, and so is full of eggs. Bowls and bowls of fresh eggs litter the tables and floor. They should be sold, but that would mean leaving the farm for a while, and I'm not sure I can do that anymore. I feel glued here, buried here, as one day I surely will be. For the moment, my in-laws are leaving us alone—I believe they think I am grieving.

One of the men, the one with the broad smile, suggests a sign to advertise sales at the entrance to the farm, says he will fix it for me and he will let me know of buyers, so I can come to the gate and sell.

'Make a little money for yourself—just for you. You could sell bread and pies, too, to day-trippers who come to be by the sea,' he says. He has kind eyes. The dirt has snuck into the creases around his eyes, making the skin seem darker there. He is nut brown from working outside in all weathers, but above the roll of his sleeves, I see a hint of white skin. What must it look like when he is naked, this two-tone body. Strange rather than attractive, I imagine.

I draw my eyes back to his smile, his question. This feels like the start of something, a step forward to financial stability, to an independence of sorts. Though it will be little, I convince myself little is all I need.

I so rarely use my voice these days, it sounds alarmingly high when I say, 'Thank you, Matthew.' I blush when I say his name. 'That would be very kind of you. Can I get you some water?'

But he has his flask, filled from the pump—he needs nothing from me. Nothing but permission.

Falling

I go for a walk alone. Just me and the dogs and the birds. The crows gather around me, protecting me from... whatever it is they still fear. I stride out. Geese gather and follow me from behind and beside, some moving ahead, but not impeding my progress. You see me coming towards you, Matthew, tilt your hat, give me that smile that I think of as a secret, though we have no secrets. We have never been truly alone—I have no idea if you even want us to be alone. But I think you do. I think you see me as I see you. Since you helped with the selling of the eggs and baking, it is as if we know each other, have formed a pact.

The geese gather tighter around me, slowing my pace, so by the time I pass you, I no longer stride, but take tiny, almost dainty steps. You stop working for a moment and watch me. I turn to you and smile back, properly, for you to see me smile for the first time. Then I redden, lose my footing, fall over the geese. I think you will reach for me, take my hand, help me up, that we will touch, but you are too busy laughing to help. I don't mind. I don't mind at all. I'll hold the sound of your laughter in my head and take it out whenever I need something warm to wrap around me.

23

Truth

My sisters have prepared a picnic for us three. Goats have already wandered over and eaten half the food and part of Esther's shawl. My sisters are laughing and singing, but when I get closer, they stop. Nudge each other, smooth out aprons and moods, clear throats, try to appear serious. It does not suit them.

'Dear Beth, do sit. Tea?' Esther says.

The tea is offered from a cracked teapot, poured into chipped cups, splashed with milk that spills everywhere. I know they want to laugh again—laughing is what they are good at—but they maintain their fake formality.

'Cake?'

I am so tired of cake. I shake my head. The dogs arrive and lick everything on the picnic blanket. At least nothing will go to waste.

'It is time, Beth,' Olivia says. Dear little Livvie, always so gentle.

'For what?' I ask.

But Livvie grows impatient and stamps her heel into the ground. 'You know. You know perfectly well. Stop this.'

But I do not know. Do not want to know. My brow creases.

It is Esther who says it. Plain-talking Esther, never one to sugarcoat anything but doughnuts. 'We are not here. We are not real. You know this, Beth. You know. It is time. It is time for you...'

I stand up and run. I hear them laugh behind me. I run for the gate, but it is not where I left it. It is never where I left it. I would leave this place—I would, I would—but when I look at my hands, I see that they are tethered to the ground. Tethered with strong twine spun from my sisters' hair. From my hair too. All twisted together, us sisters. I look back, but they are no longer beside the picnic blanket. I run to the barn, rebuilt by my husband's family, check that the new door is not blocked. I run to the house, look for them in every room. I look out of the window and see them there, at the end of the far field, standing next to the gate, waving to me. I run downstairs and am relieved to find them in the kitchen, cleaning up. They do not look at me, simply carry on as before.

I feel the world tilt, as though I am on the ship I imagined, and there is no one here to catch me. I call for my mother, but she is long gone—that much I do know—and for my father, who is with her, and would not have known how to help me. And even for my husband, lost at sea, as am I.

Burn It All Down

The cobweb-fine curtains blow in the wind, a storm gathers, the men work in the fields, the cat spits out its milk, and I knead, knead, knead the dough on the board, eight loaves already made, another proving, but still I knead, knead, knead the dough, my hair, tied up, safe, sanitary, tries to break free, the wildness in me forcing it out of ribbons and clasps and grips, and I grip, grip, grip to this life, to this kitchen, to this dough because if I let go, let it all go, let out these curls and cries, what then, what then, what then for the men who work in the fields, who work for me and all the other coiled women and ungrateful cats, so I knead, knead, knead the dough, and once, when I first saw you smile at me in the field, it felt like that half second before I save myself from falling, like a thousand tiny springs had loosened from my tight gut and risen up through my chest and out of my head, escaping my curls, and now I need, need, need, you are working in the fields when I need you, and I could knead your skin and bruise it like the berries for tomorrow's pie, because there must always be pie, and I'll scrub, scrub, scrub this place clean when the kneading and rolling and holding in and the needing and falling and failing are all forgotten, and now, when I look out to watch you work, your muscles strained, your head bowed, your shirt soaked with sweat, I wipe my own brow and smile at a tree alight in the distance, burning it all down, its cleansing fire setting us all free at last.

Dancing in the Burning Fields

In the field a ship burns, my sisters dance, dogs snarl, crows swoop and peck at my hair — hair that escapes fixings, no matter how firmly I tie it down.

In our house the windows are always open, to let everything out and everything in. My sisters bake pies — more pies than we could ever eat — the table strewn with flour, blueberries and crows. The crows dapple the rolled pastry with claw prints as they caw their demands to be fed.

In the field I run to the gate, but the gate is not there, the barn burning behind me flushes my guilty face.

In our house the dogs snarl and nip at my heels, claw at skirts, fight the crows for their share of food, while my sisters drink tea from my mother's chipped and scratched and cracked wedding china.

In the field I dream of escape, lie with my eyes closed, hear my sisters play fiddles, feel the approach of the storm that will tear us all down or wash us all clean.

In our house my sisters and I do not make eye contact. We work together in perfect time, a harmony that would break if we sought to see each other properly.

In the field my sisters gather herbs and sing our songs. I realise I no longer remember all the words.

In our house I find myself alone. I inhale the silence, exhale the peace. And then you walk in, run your fingers through my wild hair, kiss my cheek, place your hand on my belly.

In the field my sisters have reached the gate. They climb over to the other side, jump up and down, so they know I will see them, smile and wave. They link arms and walk on. My sisters are truly gone.

Acknowledgements

Many thanks to Alfie Jones, Damhnait Monaghan and Diane Simmons for being first readers. Thank you to Kathy Fish, who first introduced me to the work of the incredible artist Andrea Kowch, and who always seems to bring out the best in my writing. And, of course, thank you to Andrea Kowch for the beautiful paintings that inspired this novella-in-flash. Thank you to John Brantingham who highly commended my novella in the Bath Novella-in-Flash Award. Thank you to Ken Elkes, Jude Higgins and Damhnait Monaghan for their generous cover quotes. Thank you to the wonderful Wordfishers: Alex Reece Abbott, April Bradley, Marie Gethins, Windy Lynn Harris, Jude Higgins, Jolene McIlwain, Alice Kaltman, Damhnait Monaghan, Georgiana Nelson, Judi Walsh and Julie Zuckerman, who encourage and support me in all my writing—you are the best team ever. Thank you to the amazing Flash Mob and to the wider writing community who make social media a better place.

Previously Published:

The story *Burn It All Down* won second prize in the Fractured Lit Microfiction Competition and was published there, online, in April 2023.

Biography

Karen Jones is a flash and short fiction writer from Glasgow, Scotland. Her flashes have been nominated for Best of the Net and The Pushcart Prize, and her story "Small Mercies" is included in *Best Small Fictions 2019*. She has won first prize in the Cambridge Flash Prize, Flash 500 and Reflex Fiction and second prize in Fractured Lit's Micro Fiction Competition. Her work has been Highly Commended or shortlisted for To Hull and Back, Bath Flash Fiction and Bath Short Story Award and many others. Her novella-in-flash *When It's Not Called Making Love* is published by Ad Hoc Fiction. She is an editor for National Flash Fiction Day anthology.

Burn it All Down, a novella inspired by the wild and richly metaphorical paintings of Andrea Kowch, shows the plight of Beth, a desperately lonely woman, trapped in an isolated rural location, who creates a fantasy world it is hard to escape from. In vivid prose, as extraordinary as Kowch's paintings, Karen Jones describes a situation universal to women the world over, in the past and present, who, through poverty and oppression, teeter on the edge of survival, mentally and physically. Beth finds solace in her sisters and her animals—chickens, cows, even bees—whose lives mingle closely with hers. Her husband, whom she scarcely knows, is lost at sea, the ocean his true love. It is a hallmark of excellent writing that a reader becomes invested in a character's life. I longed for Beth to be set free and by the end of the story, it is heart-warming to believe she finds love and a way to a better future.
—Jude Higgins, author of *The Chemist's House*, V.Press

Evocative and haunting, *Burn It All Down* is a dark, edgy fairytale. In a riotous house, surrounded by memories, her free-spirited sisters and a menagerie of creatures, Beth waits for her husband's return. Karen Jones's prose soars, swoops and loops, circling back like the ever-present crows in this extraordinary novella-in-flash. This is a writer at the top of her game.
—Damhnait Monaghan, author of *New Girl in Little Cove*

The novella-in-flash is by its nature a liminal form, but that is a gift in the assured writing of Karen Jones, who uses the darkly mysterious paintings of American artist Andrea Kowch as a springboard for a compelling tale, infused with yearning, melancholy, and flashes of wry humour. This book may be small but is in no way slight. It is its own world and an insightful meditation on sisterhood and a woman's quest for freedom, while trapped in an indifferent patriarchal society.
—KM Elkes, author of *All That Is Between Us*

Printed in Great Britain
by Amazon